Gross History

Gross
FACTS About
the Middle Ages

BY MIRA VONNE

Raintree is an imprint of Capstone Global Library Limited, a company incorporated in England and Wales having its registered office at 264 Banbury Road, Oxford, OX2 7DY – Registered company number: 6695582

www.raintree.co.uk
myorders@raintree.co.uk

Edited by Mandy Robbins
Designed by Philippa Jenkins
Picture research by Wanda Winch
Production by Steve Walker
Printed and bound in China.

ISBN 978 1 4747 5215 2
21 20 19 18 17
10 9 8 7 6 5 4 3 2 1

British Library Cataloguing in Publication Data
A full catalogue record for this book is available from the British Library.

Photo Credits
Bridgeman Images: © Look and Learn/Private Collection/Michael Godfrey, cover, © Historic England/Private Collection/Judith Dobie, 17, © Look and Learn/Private Collection/English School, 29, © Look and Learn/Private Collection/Harry Green, 27, © Look and Learn/Private Collection/Pat Nicolle, 15, Biblioteca Marciana, Venice, Italy/Italian School, 19, Ken Welsh/Private Collection/André Both, 13, Natural History Museum, London, UK, 9, Photo © Tarker, 23, Private Collection/English School, 21, Victoria & Albert Museum, London, UK/Limbourg Brothers, 7; The Image Works: © Michael Siluk, 11; North Wind Picture Archives, 5; Philippa Jenkins, 24; Science Source/Colorization by Mary Martin, 25; Shutterstock: irin-k, fly design, Milan M, color splotch design, monkeystock, grunge drip design, NatureArtForest, 20, Produck, slime bubbles design, Protasov AN, weevil, Taborsky, 18

CONTENTS

Dirty work

In AD 476 the fall of the Roman **Empire** marked the start of the Middle Ages. Life in Europe at this time was difficult and gross. Most land was owned by lords. **Serfs** worked the land from dawn to dusk.

empire large territory ruled by a powerful leader

serf person who worked without pay on a certain piece of land; serfs could be sold along with the land

4

Peasants and serfs farmed by hand. This was dirty work. Most people bathed just once a week. Bath water came from nearby streams. These were the same streams people dumped rubbish and **sewage** into.

peasant poor person who owned a small farm or worked on a farm, especially in Europe during the Middle Ages

sewage human waste that is carried away in sewers and drains in modern times

Gross Fact

Peasants and serfs lived in cramped one-room houses. Farm animals would often share space with family members.

Peasants tried to stay clean.
They washed their hands several times
a day. Family members helped each
other pick off lice from their hair and
clothes. Peasants wore the same stiff,
itchy clothes every day.

Gross Fact

Some wool clothing was never
washed but simply brushed.

9

Rotten teeth

Many peasants had dirty, rotten teeth and awful breath. People didn't use toothbrushes or toothpaste. Many chewed **herbs** such as mint to cover bad breath. They also rinsed their mouths with vinegar and wine.

herb plant with qualities that can treat illness

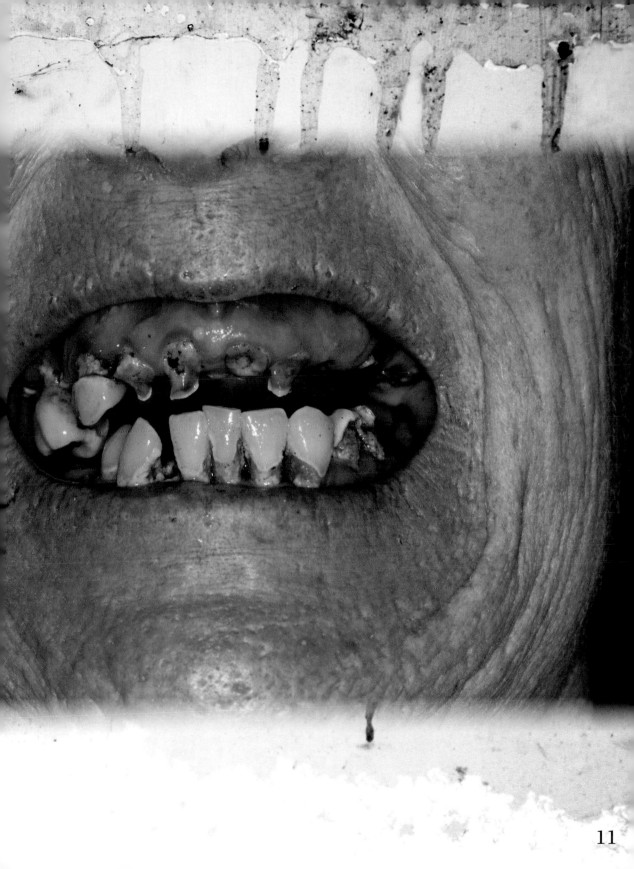

Few treatments existed for rotted teeth. Some people thought worms caused **cavities**. They tried to force out the "worms" by holding an open flame under their jaw. Most people just had their teeth yanked out with pliers.

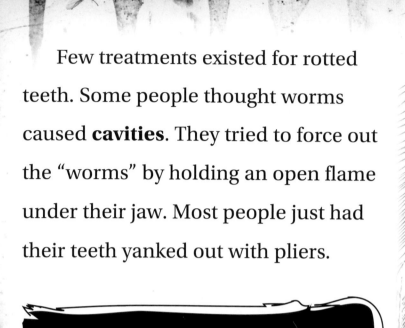

cavity decayed or broken down part of a tooth

Gross Fact

Rich patients replaced their pulled teeth with fake ones made of cow bone.

Foul food

Peasants ate whatever meat they could catch. This included rabbits, beavers and pigeons. They often dried meat to keep it from rotting. Meat was also stored in a gel made from boiled cow hooves.

Gross Fact

People didn't eat a wide variety of fruits or vegetables. The lack of vitamins left many people with loose teeth and bad gums.

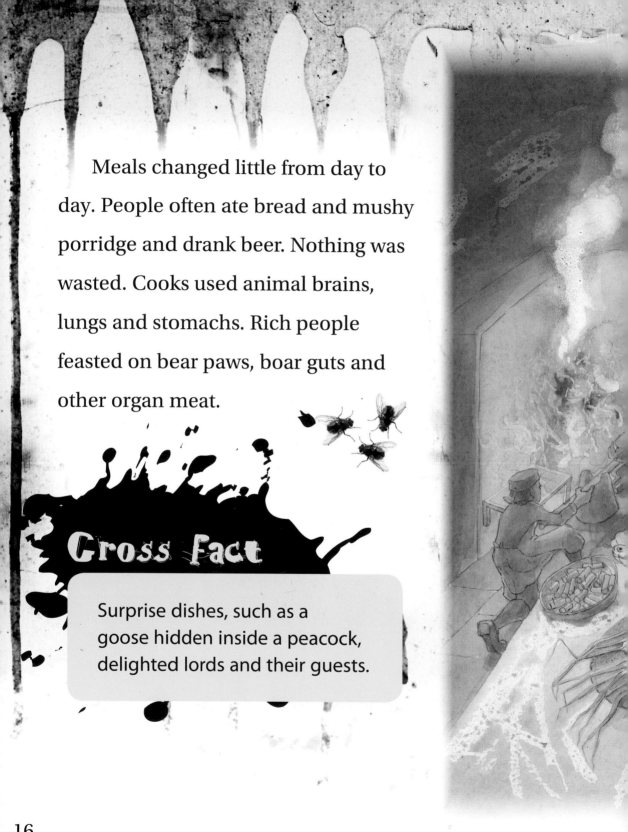

Meals changed little from day to day. People often ate bread and mushy porridge and drank beer. Nothing was wasted. Cooks used animal brains, lungs and stomachs. Rich people feasted on bear paws, boar guts and other organ meat.

Gross Fact

Surprise dishes, such as a goose hidden inside a peacock, delighted lords and their guests.

Lords sometimes ate meat on **trenchers**. These stale pieces of bread soaked up grease. After eating, the lords gave the trenchers to peasants. For peasants, the grease-soaked, stale pieces of bread were a real treat.

trencher stale bread sliced to make a plate for other food, usually meat

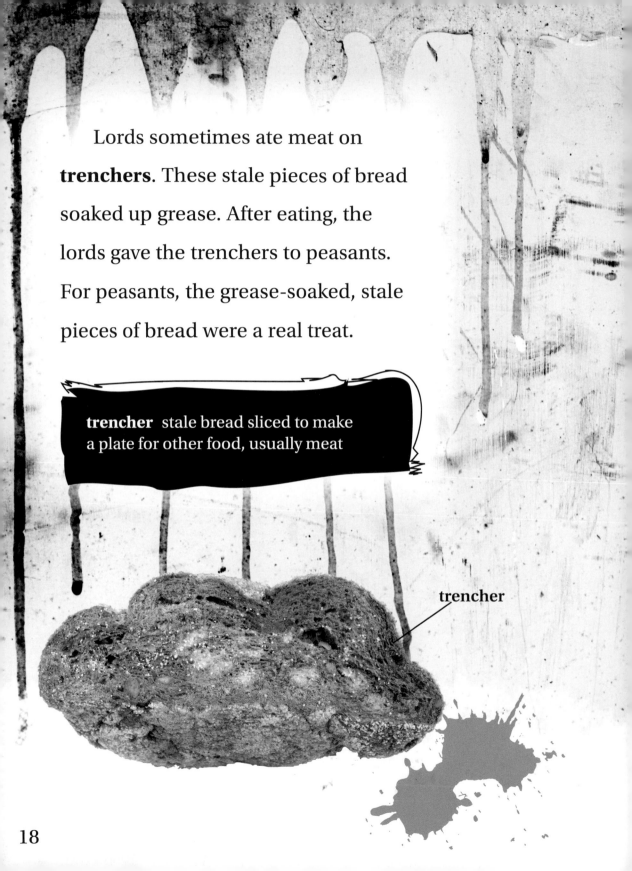

trencher

Stinking cities

Cities in the Middle Ages were crowded and smelly. Rubbish piled up in the streets along with human and animal waste. Many cities had walls around them to keep attackers out. The walls kept the stink in.

People could get sick from eating spoiled meat. Anyone caught selling rotten food had their goods burned. To ensure fresh meat, animals were **butchered** at market. Blood and guts were splattered in the street.

butcher cut up raw meat

Don't get sick!

People had little medical knowledge in the Middle Ages. Treatments included eating herbs, chanting or smearing poo on injuries. Sometimes treatments actually killed patients.

herbs

Gross Fact

One treatment for sickness was bloodletting. Doctors sliced open a person's vein to release "bad blood". The treatment could kill people.

The Black Death hit Europe in the mid-1300s. This deadly **plague** killed nearly one-third of all Europeans. The first sign was usually a small, black bump. Once the bump appeared, the plague could kill within a week.

plague very serious disease that spreads quickly to many people and often causes death

Gross Fact

People didn't know it, but they caught the plague from fleas.

The plague killed more people than survivors could bury. Bodies were left in the street or dumped in the sea. The plague proved that the Middle Ages were not just disgusting, but deadly.

Glossary

butcher cut up raw meat

cavity decayed or broken part of a tooth

empire large territory ruled by a powerful leader

herb plant with qualities that can sometimes treat illness

peasant poor person who owned a small farm or worked on a farm, especially in Europe during the Middle Ages

plague very serious disease that spreads quickly to many people and often causes death

serf person who worked without pay on a certain piece of land; serfs could be sold along with the land

sewage human waste that is carried away in sewers and drains in modern times

trencher stale bread sliced to make a plate for other food, usually meat

Read more

Measly Middle Ages (Horrible Histories), Terry Deary (Scholastic, 2016)

The Middle Ages (History of Britain), Abigail Wheatley (Usborne, 2015)

The Middle Ages (The Gruesome Truth About), Matt Buckingham (Wayland, 2012)

Websites

www.ducksters.com/history/middle_ages_timeline.php
Lots of information about life in the Middle Ages, including a timeline.

www.historyforkids.net/middle-ages.html
Visit this website to find out about the Middle Ages with quizzes to test your knowledge.

Comprehension questions

- How did people in the Middle Ages end up drinking contaminated water?

- Peoples' diets were very different in the Middle Ages. Compare and contrast what people ate back then to what they eat today.

Index